ICDL®/ECDL®

Databases

Using Microsoft® Access

Syllabus Version 6.0

Published by: **Conor Jordan**

Arthurstown

New Ross

Co. Wexford

E-mail: conorjordan@gmail.com

Web: www.digidiscover.com

The intent of this manual is to provide a guide to students and teachers to help them understand the current ICDL syllabus and the features associated with using the application as part of the curriculum.

Conor Jordan does not guarantee students will pass their respective exams as a result of reading this manual. Its purpose is to enable students to gain a greater understanding of the application which may or may not help them achieve their desired results in exams.

Revision sections are for practice purposes only and are not official ICDL tests. Sample tests for each module can be downloaded from the ICDL website to prepare students for their exams.

Aims

The aim of this manual is to give students and teachers a clear understanding of the advanced features and functions of Microsoft Word required for Advanced ICDL certification. It aims to achieve this by providing a step-by-step tutorial designed to provide learners with the skills required to use the advanced elements of the application.

Objectives

On completion of this manual, learners should be able to:

- Understand what a database is and how it functions
- Create a database and view the database using different methods
- Create a table, adjust field property settings and input data into a table
- Sort and filter and table and form
- Run queries to extract information from a database
- Understand and create forms, modify and delete records
- Create reports and prepare printouts

Downloading the Work Files

Work files associated with this manual provides the opportunity to practice the techniques outlined without having to type and format many documents saving the learner time to focus on the practical exercises. An internet connection is required to download the files. Visit www.digidiscover.com/downloads and click on the manual you are using.

Files should be saved in an ECDL folder in your Documents folder on your computer.

Contents

Section 1 – Introduction

Introduction

A database contains information stored in tables e.g. a telephone directory. Each table should contain information on a single subject. Changes to tables are automatically saved in Access. Information is the result of a process that outputs data using Access.

Tables can be linked together to create a large database. A **Field** is a **Column** of data that should contain one element of data. A **Record** is each **Row** of related data such as Name, Address and Telephone number and should have data relating to a single subject.

Data can be displayed in a **Form** that shows one record on screen at a time. Data can be represented in a **Report** allowing the user to perform calculations and print out information in an easy to understand way

Queries allows users to ask questions of the database and show information based on those questions. Common uses of databases include: Government records, Customer Details records, Financial Account records and social networks

Databases are used by a range of organisations such as banks to maintain records of accounts, hospitals to keep patient information and e-commerce websites to store product information.

Starting Access

1. Click on the **Start** button
2. Locate the **Access** application in the list of apps
3. Click on the **Access** application

⌄ **New**

Blank database

4. Click on **Blank Database**

5. Click on the **Create** button

The Access Screen

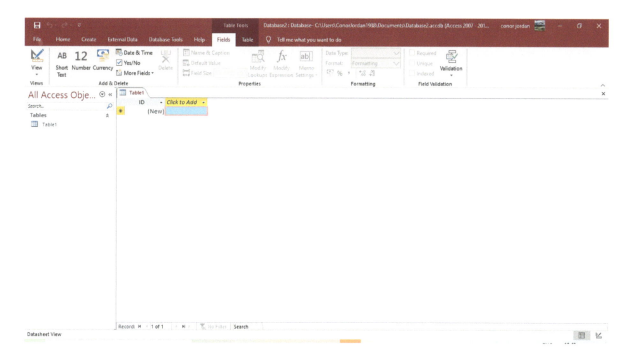

The **Title Bar** provides information about the database name and where it's located on your computer

The **Ribbon** contains a collection of **Tabs** divided into **Groups** which contains buttons that perform different functions

Hover your mouse pointer over a button to read a description of it **(ToolTip)**

The **Navigation Pane** on the left-hand side of the screen allows you to **Open**, **Edit**, **Rename** and **Delete** objects in the database

The **Access Window** is where objects are created, edited or displayed

Some buttons produce an immediate effect such as the **Filter** button

Change the view by clicking on the **View** button and choosing **Design View**

Design View allows the design of the table to be changed

View

Views

Some buttons turn effects on and off such as the **Property Sheet** button in **Design View**

Other buttons give further options using drop-down menus such as the **View** button

Click on a **Dialog Box Launcher** to display a **Dialog Box**

A **Dialog Box** allows information to be entered into it

Click on the **Small Chevron** to hide the **Ribbon** from view

Click on a tab such as the **Home** tab

Click on the **Pin the Ribbon** button to reveal the **Ribbon**

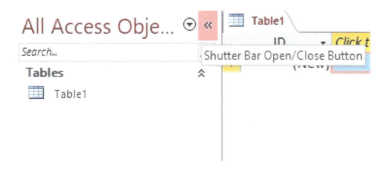

Click on the Shutter Bar Open/Close Button to hide the All Access Objects pane

Click on this button again to reveal the All Access Objects Pane

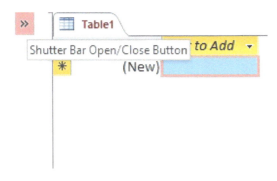

Quick Access Toolbar

The **Quick Access Toolbar** is located on the top-left of the screen

It contains buttons that perform different functions

The **Save** button allows you to save the database using the same file name

The **Undo** button allows you to Undo a task

The **Arrow** beside the **Undo** button allows you to undo a number of tasks

Redo allows you to reverse an Undo

The arrow beside the **Redo** button allows you to Redo a number of tasks

The **Customize Quick Access Toolbar** allows you to choose what appears on the **Quick Access Toolbar**

Opening, Closing & Saving

1. Click on the **File** tab

2. Click on the **Save As** option

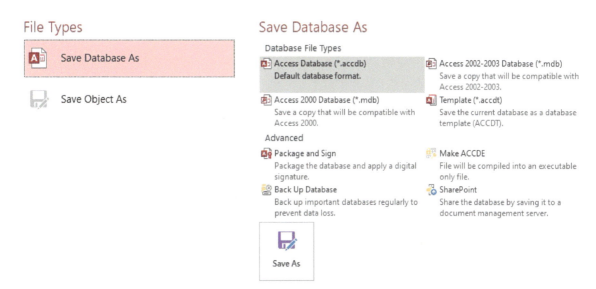

3. Click on the **Save As** button

4. Navigate to the folder you want to save your database

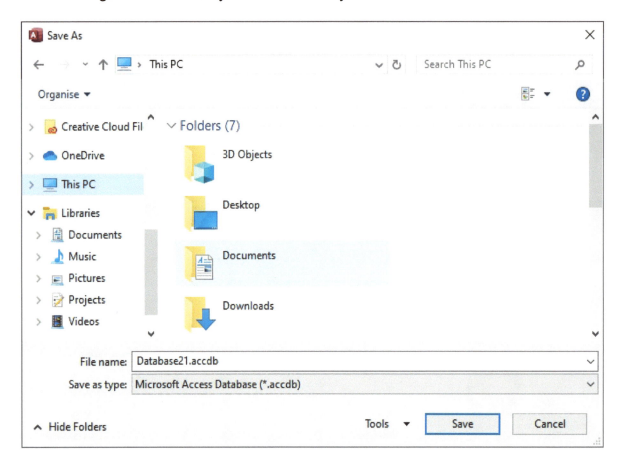

5. Name your database in the **File Name** text box
6. Click on the **Save** button

Closing a Database

1. Click on the **File** tab

2. Click on the **Close** option
3. To close the **Access** application, click on the **Close** button on the top-right hand corner of the screen

Closing a Table

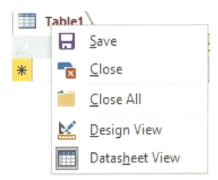

1. Right-click on the tab of a table
2. Select **Close** to close the table

Open a Database

1. Click on the **File** tab

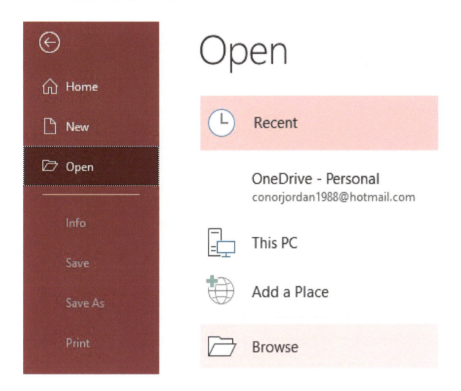

2. Click on the **Open** option
3. Select **This PC**
4. Click on the **Browse** button

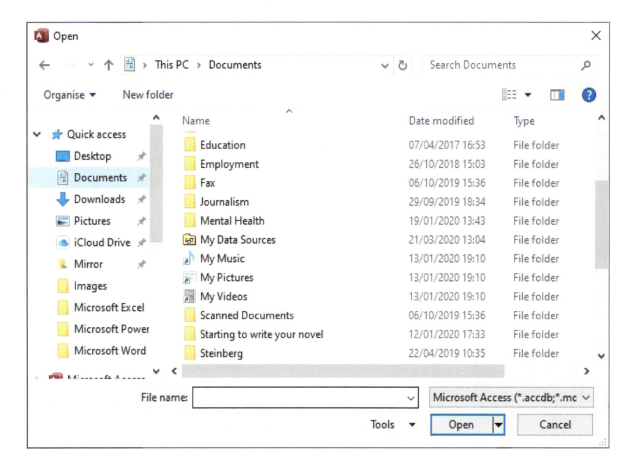

5. Locate the database

6. Select the database

7. Click on the **Open** button

Help

1. Click on the **Help** tab

2. In the **Help** group, click on **Help**

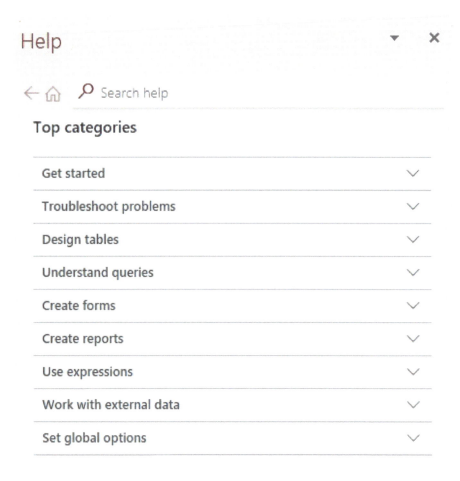

3. Type in the **Search Help** search bar to find a topic you need help with
4. Click on **Get Started** to learn about the basics of **Access**
5. Click on the **Back Arrow** to return to the previous topic
6. Click on the **Home** icon to return to this pane

7. In the **Tell Me** box, type in what task you want to perform e.g. Save

8. Choose the **Save** option
9. You will be prompted to save the table

Revision Section 1

1. What is a field in a database?
2. What is a row in a database?
3. What is the purpose of a form?
4. What is a report in Access?
5. What is the purpose of a query?
6. What type of organisations use databases?
7. Create a blank database?
8. Hide the ribbon from view.
9. Display the ribbon again?
10. Use the quick access toolbar to save the database as 'Records'
11. Close the database
12. Navigate to the work files folder and open the 'Records' database
13. Use the help function to find information about how to create a table
14. Save and close the 'Records' database

Section 2 - Tables

Moving Around a Table

On the bottom of the **Datasheet View** there are **Navigation** buttons to allow you to move through records in a database. This allows you to display records in a database so they can be edited. This is a useful feature in Access as it allows the user to search records.

1. Click on the **Next Record** button to move to the next record

2. Click on the **Previous Record** button to move to the previous record

3. Click on the **Last Record** button to move to the last record

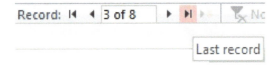

4. Click on the **First Record** button to move to the first record

5. On the **Home** tab in the **Find** group, click on **Go To**

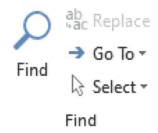

Find

ab
↵ac Replace

→ Go To ▾

⬚ Select ▾

Find

6. You can select to navigate through the records from here

Moving with the Keyboard

1. The **Arrow** Keys can be used to move up, down, left & right
2. The **End** key moves to the end of a record
3. The **Home** key moves to the start of a record
4. The **Tab** key moves one column to the right

Creating a Table

Field Names (Column Headers) and Data Types are created when making a table.
The Data Type must be suitable for what will be entered into that field.

Types of data include:

Text – Allows text and numbers to be entered

Number – Allows only numbers

Currency – Includes a Currency sign and decimal point

Date/Time – Includes date and time formats

Yes/No – Displayed as Yes/No, True/False

1. Open a blank database
2. On the **Home** tab in the **Views** group, click on **View**

View

Views

3. The table will be opened in **Design View**
4. Enter the following information:

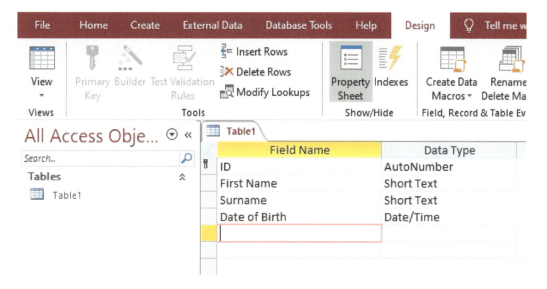

5. Select the **Data Type** using the drop-down menu

6. You can also type in a brief **Description** of the **Field**

7. You may type in a **Description** for the **First Name** field as:

8. "Enter first name"

9. Right-click on the **Table1** tab

10. Select **Save**

11. Enter **Customers** in the **Table Name** text box

12. Click **OK**

13. Save the database as 'Customer Details' and leave it open

Entering Data

Information can be entered into a database. This may be employee records, contact details or product information. This has to be done manually by the user.

1. Open the 'Customer Details' database
2. On the **Table Tools Design Tab** in the **Views** group, click on **View** to return to **Datasheet View**

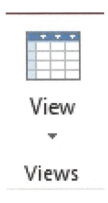

View

Views

3. Notice the **Field Names** are now column headers
4. Enter in the following information:

ID	First Name	Surname	Date of Birth
1 John	Smith	04/05/1998	
2 Mary	Joyce	12/04/2007	
3 George	Hughes	05/07/1997	
4 Tom	McGrath	25/08/1987	
(New) Enter Name			

5. Use the **Tab** key or the Enter key to move right
6. You can delete the contents of a record by clicking inside a record and pressing the backspace key
7. Type in the record to modify the data
8. Save the database and leave it open

Format Field Properties

There are a variety of field properties that can be adjusted to format fields in a database. This changes how the data in the field will appear. Depending on the information required in each field, the user can choose from a number of different format options.

1. Open the 'Customer Details' database
2. Click on the **First Name Field** in the **Field** Column

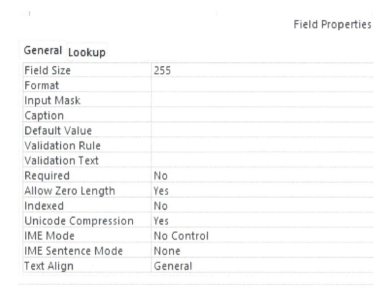

3. The **Field Properties** appear at the bottom of the screen
4. Click on the **Field Size** property
5. Change the number to 30
6. This will only allow 30 characters to be entered into this **Field**
7. Click on the **Date of Birth** Field Name

8. Click on the **Format Property** for this field

9. Choose **Long Date** from the drop-down menu

10. This will change the **Format** of the **Date of Birth** field

11. Click on the **ID Field Name**

12. Click on the **Format Property** for this field

13. Select **Long Integer** from the drop-down menu

14. Click on the **First Name Field Name**

General Lookup

Field Size	255
Format	
Input Mask	
Caption	
Default Value	`Enter Name` ...
Validation Rule	
Validation Text	
Required	No
Allow Zero Length	Yes
Indexed	No
Unicode Compression	Yes
IME Mode	No Control
IME Sentence Mode	None
Text Align	General

15. Click on the **Default Value** for this Field

16. Type "Enter Name"

17. This will make this text appear in this column before any information is entered

18. Save the database

Primary Key

A Primary Key is used to uniquely identify each record in a table. This is used when your database has more than one tables. Relationships between tables can be made using a primary key linking similar fields.

1. Open the 'Customer Details' database
2. Click in the ID **Field Name**

3. On the **Table Tools Design** tab in the **Tools** group, select the **Primary Key** button
4. This will sort the records in numerical order by **ID**
5. Save the database and leave it open

Indexes

An Index makes finding data in a table easier and speeds up search queries. In a Telephone Directory, phone numbers are indexed to make finding a phone number easier. The table will be sorted by the field that is indexed.

1. Open the 'Customer Details' database
2. Click on the **Surname** field name

General Lookup

Field Size	255
Format	
Input Mask	
Caption	
Default Value	
Validation Rule	
Validation Text	
Required	No
Allow Zero Length	Yes
Indexed	Yes (No Duplicates)
Unicode Compression	Yes
IME Mode	No Control
IME Sentence Mode	None
Text Align	General

3. Under **Filed Properties** click on the **Indexed** drop-down menu and choose **Yes (No Duplicates)**
4. This will only allow surnames to appear **Once** and will sort the table in alphabetical order **by surname**
5. Switch to **Datasheet View** to display the sorted table
6. Switch back to Design View
7. On the **Table Tools Design** tab in the **Show/Hide** group, click on **Indexes**

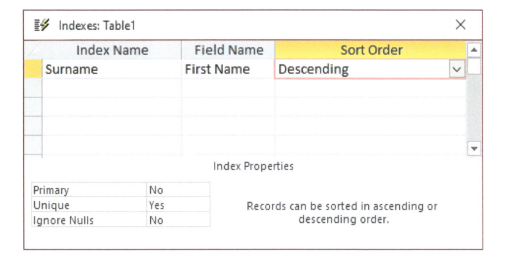

8. Select **First Name** in the **Field Name** Column

9. Choose **Descending** in the **Sort Order** column

10. Close the **Indexes** dialog box and switch to **Datasheet View**

11. The table is now sorted by **First Name** in **Descending** order

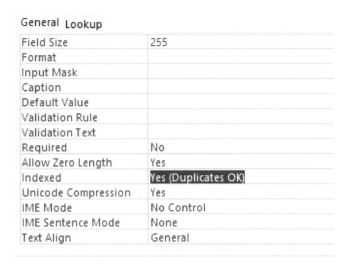

12. Under **Field Properties** click on the **Indexed** drop-down menu

13. Choose **Yes (Duplicates OK)**

14. This will allow you to enter the same surname more than once in the table

15. Save the database as 'Customer Details'

Validation Rules

This sets out what must be entered into a field. This feature prevents incorrect information being entered into a field. The user can set validation rules to prevent mistakes occurring during the information input process.

1. Open the 'Customer Details' database
2. Right-click to the left of the First Name field name
3. Choose **Insert Rows**

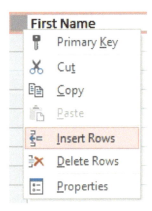

4. Type in **Title** as the Field Name and **Short Text** as the Data Type
5. Click on the **Validation Rule** field property
6. Type in Mr or Mrs or Ms
7. This will only allow these titles to be entered into that filed
8. Switch to **Datasheet View** and try typing Miss
9. Access will not allow you to enter that title because of the **Validation Rule**
10. Enter in "Telephone No" as a **Field Name** and **Number** as the **Data Type**
11. In the **Validation Rule** for this field type in Like #######
12. This will ensure that 7 numbers must be entered into the Telephone No field
13. Save the database as 'Validation Rule'

To Delete a Field

1. Select a **Field** in **Design View**
2. In the **Tools** group, select **Delete Rows**
3. A row has been deleted

Printing a Table

Tables can be printed in Access to produce a hard copy of the information entered into a table.

1. On the **File** tab click on the **Print** option
2. Choose **Print Preview** to view a preview of the table
3. Click on the preview to zoom in
4. Click again to zoom out
5. In the **Page Layout** group, select **Landscape** to change the page orientation

6. In the **Page Size** group, click on the **Size** button and select **Legal**

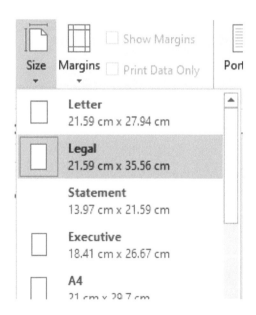

7. In the **Print** group, click on the **Print** button

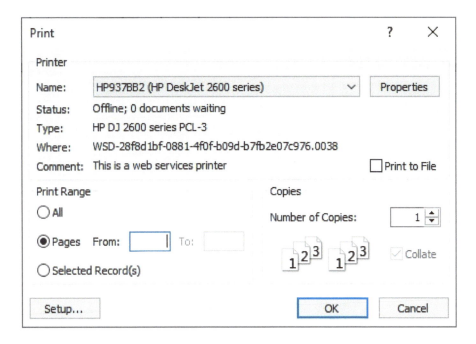

8. Under Print Range, select All to print the entire table

9. Under **Print Range**, select **Pages** and choose what pages you want printed e.g. From 2 To 4

10. Select a range of records by clicking and dragging to the left of the table

11. This will select a number of rows

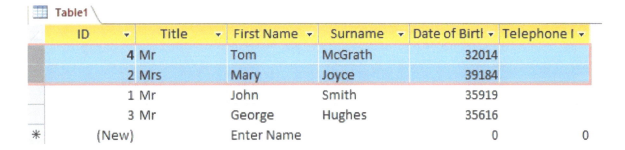

ID	Title	First Name	Surname	Date of Birtl	Telephone I
4	Mr	Tom	McGrath	32014	
2	Mrs	Mary	Joyce	39184	
1	Mr	John	Smith	35919	
3	Mr	George	Hughes	35616	
(New)		Enter Name		0	0

12. Return to the **Print Preview** screen and click on the **Print** button

13. Choose **Selected Records** to print only the **Selected Records** in a database

14. Click **OK** to print the selected range

15. Save the database and leave it open

Delete a Table

1. Close the table you want to delete
2. Right-click on the **Table** in the **Navigation Pane** you want to delete
3. Choose **Delete**

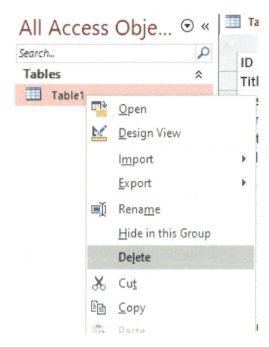

Revision Section 2

1. Open the 'Contact Details' database
2. Move to record 3 within the 'Mailing' table
3. Use the 'Go To' tool to the post code 'UY26DR4'
4. Use the arrow keys to move to the end of record 3
5. Create a new table called 'Customers'
6. In Design View, enter the following Field Names:
   - ID   AutoNumber
   - Title   Short Text
   - First Name   Short Text
   - Surname   Short Text
   - Date of Birth   Date/Time
7. Enter the following information into the table:
   - 1   Mr   Sean   James   4/5/87
   - 2   Mrs   Lisa   Smith   23/6/89
   - 3   Mr   Richard   Dunne   31/3/85
   - 4   Mrs   Mary   Kelly   28/8/91
8. Format the Date of Birth field to have a Medium Date
9. Apply a Default Value of 'Enter Surname' for the Surname field
10. Apply a Primary Key to the ID field
11. Apply an index of 'Yes (No Duplicates) to the Date of Birth field
12. Sort the table by Surname Ascending
13. Apply a Validation Rule to the Title field with the text 'Mr, Mrs or Ms'
14. Delete the Date of Birth field
15. Print the table in landscape view
16. Delete the 'Mailing' table
17. Save the database as 'Postal Applicants'

Section 3 – Relationships

About Relationships

Tables in a database can be related so that information is not duplicated. You could have a **Customer Details** table that contains the contact information for each customer. This could be related to an **Orders** table providing details of every order that was made. Rather than having to repeat the customer details for every order, you can create a **One-To-Many** relationship so that one record in the **Customer Details** table is related to many records in the **Orders** table. This is because some customers are likely to order more than one product from a company

Tables are related using **Key Fields**

The first table will likely have the **Primary Key**

The matching field in the other table will have the **Foreign Key**

Creating Relationships

Access allows you to link tables together so that records are maintained. For example, a primary table containing information about Customers may be linked to Products Ordered. This will establish a link between customer details and the products they have ordered.

1. Create a table called 'Customer Details' with the following field names:
2. Customer Ref, First Name, Surname, Address, Telephone No.
3. Fill in the details for each customer

4. Create another table called **Orders** with the following field names:
5. Order Ref, Customer Ref, Order Date & Order Cost
6. Fill in the details for each order making sure some customers order more than one product

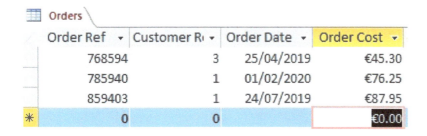

7. Save the database and leave it open

One-to-Many Relationships

A one-to-many relationship is when a primary table containing one field of data is linked to a table with all the details for that field. For example, a table containing Contact Details can be held in one table and can be related to a Company table where all of the details for that company are held only once.

1. Open the 'Customer Details' database
2. On the **Database Tools** tab in the **Relationships** group, click on **Relationships**

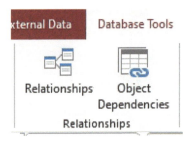

3. In the **Show Table** dialog box, select the **Customer Details** table and click on **Add**
4. Do the same for the **Orders** table
5. Click and drag the **Customer Ref** field in the **Customer Details** table to the **Customer Ref** field in the **Orders** table
6. In the **Edit Relationships** dialog box, click on the **Create** button

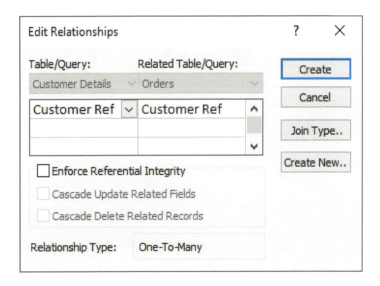

7. A **One-To-Many** relationship type is created

8. Return to the **Customer Details** table

9. Click on the **Expand** symbol to reveal the order details related to Stephen
   Dunne

10. This is called a **Subdatasheet**

11. Save the database

Enforcing Referential Integrity

This prevents **Primary Key** data in the main table from being changed or deleted or any data being changed or deleted in the **Primary Table.** In this example, **Enforcing Referential Integrity** will prevent details in the **Customer Details** table from being deleted or changed and data in the **Customer Ref** field for both tables from being changed or deleted

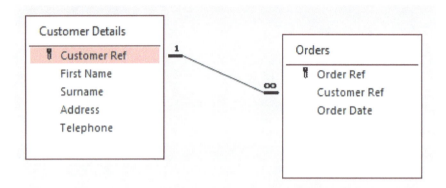

1. Open the 'Customer Details' database
2. Right-click on the relationship between both tables
3. Choose **Edit Relationship**
4. Click on the **Enforce Referential Integrity** checkbox
5. Click **OK**
6. Save the database and leave it open

Update & Delete Records

Records in a table can be updated whenever a change has been made to the information contained within a table. Records can also be deleted if they are deemed unnecessary.

1. On the **Database Tools** tab, click on the **Relationships** button
2. Right-click on the relationship between both tables
3. Choose **Edit Relationship**
4. Click on the checkbox for **Cascade Update Related Fields**
5. Click on the checkbox for **Cascade Delete Related Records**
6. Click **OK**
7. This will allow you to update and delete records in these tables
8. Any changes made will be shown in the **Orders** table
9. Enter a new record in the **Customer Details** table

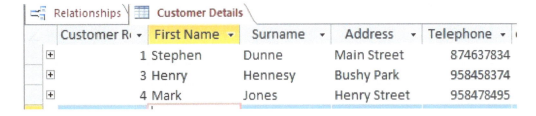

10. Delete the second record in the **Customer Details** table by right-clicking to the left of the record and choosing **Delete Record**

11. You can use an alternative method to update and delete records
12. On the **Home** tab in the **Records** group, click on **New** to create a new record
13. In the **Records** group, click on **Delete** to delete a selected record
14. You can use the keyboard shortcut **Ctrl+'** (Apostrophe) to copy the previous record
15. Insert the current date by using the keyboard shortcut **Ctrl+;** (Semi-Colon)

Access

Deleting a Relationship

Sometimes it will be necessary to delete a relationship. This is when the user no longer wants to maintain a link between tables.

1. Open the **Relationships** window

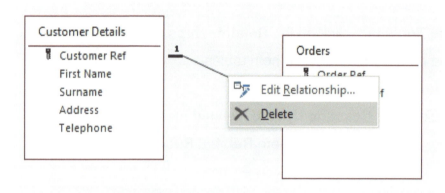

2. Right-click on the line joining both tables
3. Choose **Delete**
4. Click on **Yes**

Revision Section 3

1. Open the database 'Clients'
2. Create a one-to-many relationship between the 'People' and 'Products' tables
3. Use the ID fields in both tables to create the relationship
4. Enforce referential integrity between both tables
5. Return to the 'People' table
6. Expand the Sarah Dunne Subdatasheet
7. Return to the relationship between both tables
8. Apply the Cascade Update Related Fields setting to the relationship
9. Apply the Cascade Delete Related Records setting to the relationship
10. Delete the relationship
11. Save the database as 'Customer Products'

Section 4 – Database Tools

Finding Text

The Find feature in Access can be used to search a database for text that matches the search criteria. This can be used to find specific details such as a company name within a table or the surname of a customer in a database.

1. Open the 'Staff Training' database
2. On the 'Staff' table, click in the **First Name** field
3. On the **Home** tab in the **Find** group, click on the **Find** button

4. In the **Find What** text box, type in Henry

5. Click on **Find Next**
6. Henry's record will be highlighted
7. In the **Find What** text box, type in Programmer
8. The record will be highlighted
9. Open the 'Courses' table

10. On the **Home** tab in the **Find** group, click on the **Find** button

11. Enter the following date into the **Find What** text box

12. Click on the **Find Next** button

13. The record with the 1/2/2020 date will be highlighted

14. Save the database and leave it open

Column Widths

Column widths can be adjusted to suit the contents of a table. This is useful when the user wants to display the information in a table so that data does not remain hidden.

1. With the 'Staff' table open, hover the mouse pointer over the division between the **Position** column and **Date of Employment** column
2. Click and drag to increase the column width to show the details within the position column
3. Select the first three columns by clicking and dragging over the column headers
4. Right-click on the headers and select **Field Width**
5. Enter 12 into the **Column Width** box
6. Click **OK**
7. All of the selected columns are measured using the same width
8. Save the database and leave it open

Wildcards

You can use three wildcards to help search a database. This is useful when you do not know the exact text or numbers contained within the record you are searching for.

? represents a single letter

* represents a group of characters

represents a single number

1. With the 'Staff' table open, select the **Find** button
2. In the **Find What** text box type in S???hen
3. Click the **Find Next** button
4. The record for Stephen Dunne is highlighted
5. Type in *k into the **Find What** text box
6. Click the **Find Next** button
7. The Mark Jones record will be highlighted
8. Click in the **Employee No** column
9. In the **Find What** text box, type in 8##
10. The employee number starting with 8 will be highlighted
11. Save the database and leave it open

Revision Section 4

1. Open the 'Staff Training' database
2. Display the 'Staff' table
3. Find the member of staff who is a Sales Representative
4. Find the employee with a date of birth of 01/08/1981
5. Open the 'Courses' table
6. Adjust the column width of the Course column so the information can be displayed
7. Use a wildcard search of find the course beginning with M
8. Save the database as 'Search' and close it

Section 5 – Sorting & Filtering

Sort & Filter

A table can be sorted in alphabetical order ascending or descending. It can also be sorted by numbers starting from the highest to the lowest or vice versa. Filters can be applied to tables to display certain details within the table.

1. Open the 'Coaches' Database containing the **Coaches** table
2. Click in the **First Name** field

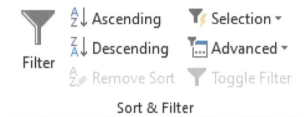

3. On the **Home** tab in the **Sort & Filter** group, select **Ascending**
4. The table will be sorted by the First Name field in ascending order
5. With the **First Name** field still selected, select **Descending** from the **Sort & Filter** group
6. The table is now sorted by the **First Name** field in descending order
7. Save the table and leave it open

Filters

Filters allow you to display data you specify in a table. This feature allows the user to analyse information contained within a table according to certain criteria.

1. Select the **Surname** column in the first record

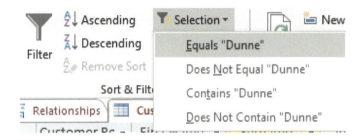

2. In the **Sort & Filter** group, click on **Selection**

3. Choose **Equals "Dunne"**

4. Only records that contain a surname Dunne will be displayed

5. Click on the **Toggle Filter** button to remove the sort

6. In the **Sort & Filter** group click on **Selection**

7. Select **Does Not Equal Dunne**

8. This will display every record that does not have **Dunne** as a **Surname**

9. Save the table and leave it open

Quick Filter

A quick filter allows you to filter records contained within a table quickly. This feature is an efficient way of displaying records that meet certain criteria.

1. Click on the drop-down arrow on the right of the **Surname** column

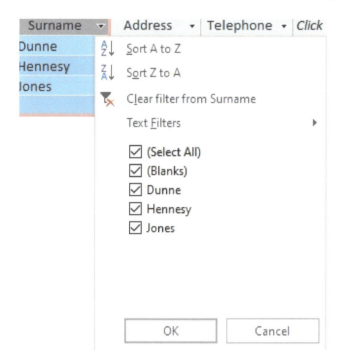

2. Click on the Hennessey checkbox

3. Click **OK**

4. Hennessey's record is not shown

5. Click on **Toggle Filter** to remove this filter

6. Click on the drop-down arrow on the right of the **First Name** column

7. Click on the **William** checkbox

8. Click **OK**

9. The record contain **William** is not shown

10. Save the table and leave it open

Advanced Filter

An advanced filter can be applied to display information that only meets certain specified criteria. This is a useful feature that allows you to show only the information you want to see.

1. Click inside the **First Name** column
2. On the **Home** tab in the **Sort & Filter** group, click on the **Advanced** button

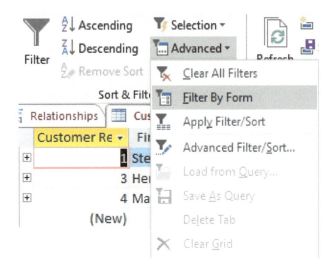

3. Choose **Filter By Form**
4. Click on the drop-down arrow in the **First Name** column and choose **Henry**
5. Click on **Toggle Filter** to apply this filter
6. Only Henry's record is shown
7. Select **Toggle Filter** again to remove this filter
8. Click inside the **Registration** column
9. On the **Home** tab in the **Sort & Filter** group, click on the **Advanced** button
10. Choose **Filter By Form**
11. Click on the drop-down arrow in the **Registration** column and choose **109F**
12. Click on **Toggle Filter** to apply this filter
13. Only the record with a registration of 109F is shown
14. Save the table and leave it open

Revision Section 5

1. Open the 'Coaches' database
2. Sort the table in descending alphabetical order by Surname
3. Display only the record that contains the Surname 'Smith'
4. Display only the records that do not contain the First Name 'George'
5. Use the Quick Filter feature to remove drivers with surnames of 'Brennan'
6. Apply an Advanced Filter to the table to display the Registration of 384M
7. Save the database as 'Sort & Filter'

Section 6 – Forms

Creating Forms

Forms display one record on screen with all of the fields associated with it. Forms can be prepared for printing so the user will have a printed copy of the records contained within a database. Pictures and text can be added to forms to make them more informative and appealing. Forms can be changed and adjusted to suit the user's preferences by adding and editing records

1. Open the 'Relationships' database
2. Click on the **Customer Details** table
3. On the **Create** tab in the **Forms** group, click on the **Form** button

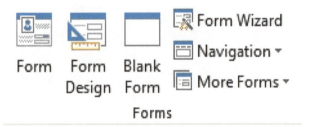

4. A Form is created based on the **Customer Details** table
5. On the **Create** tab in the **Forms** group, click on **More Forms**
6. Choose **Split Form** from the options available

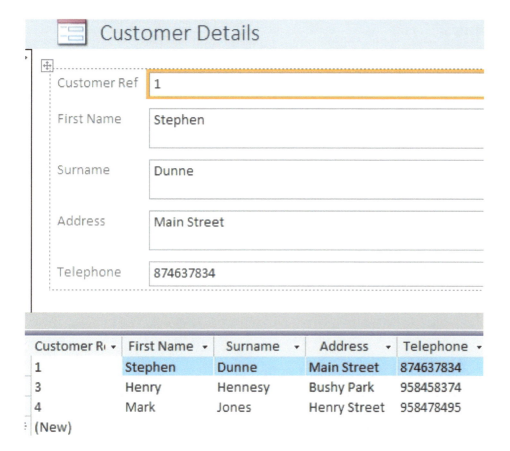

7. The table can now be viewed beneath the form

8. Save the form as 'Customer Details' and leave it open

Navigating Forms

Users can move between forms using the navigation tools at the bottom of the form window. Access allows the user to view different form records.

1. At the bottom of the form window, click on the **Next** button to move through the records

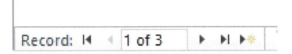

2. On the right, click on the **New Record** button
3. Enter details into the **Form**
4. Click on the **Previous** button to move back through records
5. Click on the **Last Record** button to move to the last record
6. Click on the **First Record** button to move to the first record
7. On the **Home** tab in the **Records** group, select **Delete** to delete a record

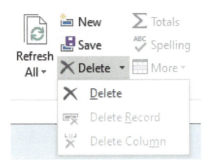

8. Right-click on the **Form Tab** and choose save
9. Right-click and choose **Close** to close the Form
10. Double-click on the **Form** on the **All Access Objects Pane** to open the form
11. Leave the database open

Form Wizard

The form wizard allows you to build forms step by step. Enter in the details you want to include in each form and access will create a form based on those details. This is an easier way of creating forms.

1. On the **Create** tab in the **Forms** group, click on **Form Wizard**

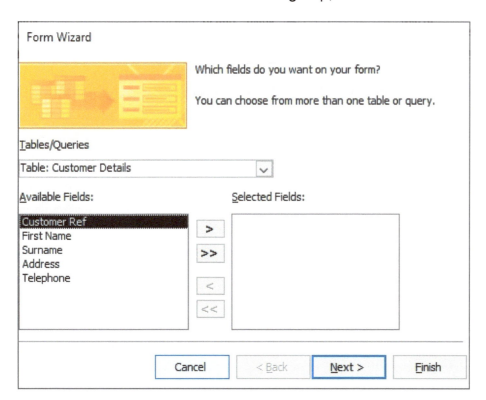

2. Make sure the **Customer Details** table is selected
3. Click on the double arrow to select all available fields
4. Click on **Next**

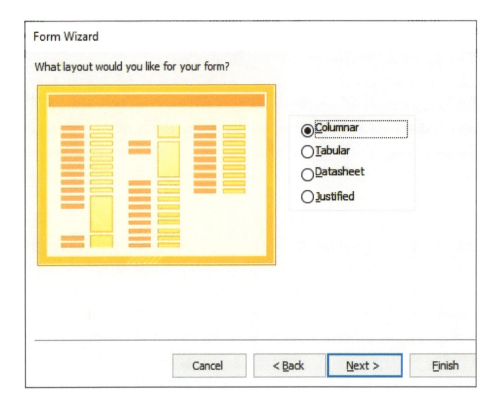

5. Select **Columnar** and click **Next**

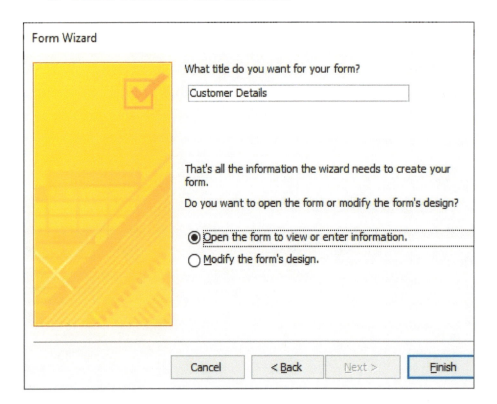

6. Click on the **Finish** button
7. The form has now been created
8. Close the form and leave the database open

Form Design

When a user wants to design a form based on specific specifications, the Form Design feature can be used. This allows the user to have greater control over how information will be displayed within a form.

1. Select the **Orders** table
2. On the **Create** tab in the **Forms** design group, click on **Form Design**

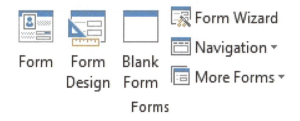

3. On the **Field List** pane on the right, click on **Show All Tables**
4. Expand the **Orders** table to view the fields
5. Click and drag each field onto the **Form Design Area**
6. Click and drag around each field to select each field (or press **Ctrl+A**)
7. Click and drag to move the fields to the centre of the form
8. Right-click in the form area
9. Choose **Form Header and Footer**
10. On the **Design** tab in the **Controls** group, select the **Label** symbol

Controls

11. Click and drag to place a title for the form in the header
12. Type in "Orders"
13. Highlight the text and on the **Format** tab in the **Font** group, make the text **Arial, bold, 16pt and centred**
14. Switch to **Form View** to see the changes made

Form Filter

Forms can be filtered to show only records that meet certain conditions. This feature is used to display forms that only meet specified criteria.

1. Click on the **First Name** Stephen
2. On the **Home** tab in the **Sort & Filter** group, click on **Selection**
3. Choose **Equals Stephen**
4. This will only display this record
5. Click on **Toggle Filter** to remove this filter

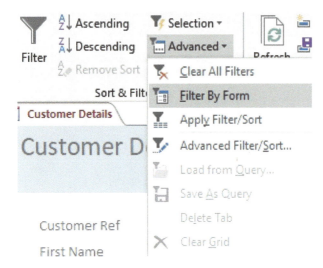

6. In the **Sort & Filter** group, select **Advanced** and choose **Filter By Form**
7. In the **First Name** field, choose **Mark**
8. Select **Toggle Filter**
9. Mark's record will be displayed
10. Leave the form open

Print a Form

A form can be printed allowing the user to obtain a copy of the records contained within a database.

1. On the **File** tab choose **Print**
2. Select **Print Preview**

3. In the **Page Layout** group select **Landscape**

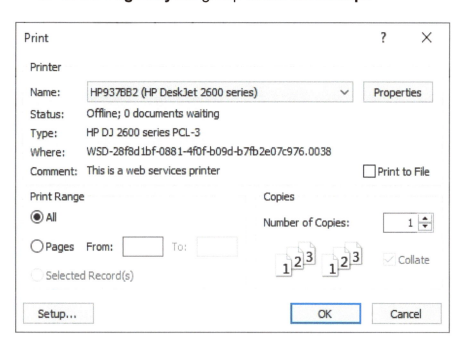

4. Under **Print Range** choose to print the entire form by selecting **All**
5. Or select **Pages** and enter in a number to start printing from that page
6. Click **OK** to print the **Form**
7. Leave the form open

Delete a Form

When a form is no longer required, it can be deleted. This will permanently remove the form from the database and cannot be retrieved.

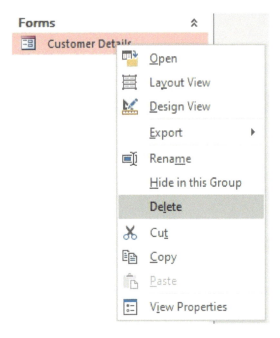

1. Right-click on the **Customer Details** Form
2. Choose **Delete**
3. Select **Yes**
4. The form has now been deleted

Revision Section 6

1. Open the 'Computer Sales' database
2. Create a form using the Form Wizard based on the 'Computers' table
3. Include all of the available fields in the form
4. Choose a Columnar layout for the form
5. Name the form 'Computers'
6. Display the TechZ computer on the form
7. Filter the form to display only computers manufactured in 2019
8. Print the form in Portrait layout
9. Delete the form after it has been printed
10. Save the database as 'Computer Details'

Section 7 – Queries

A Query extracts selected fields and records from tables allowing you to analyse the results. You can choose what fields to include in a Query and specify what conditions need to be met for records to be displayed. This is a quick way of extracting data from a database allowing the user to analyse the information.

1. Open the 'Client Orders' database
2. On the **Create** tab in the **Queries** group, select **Query Design**

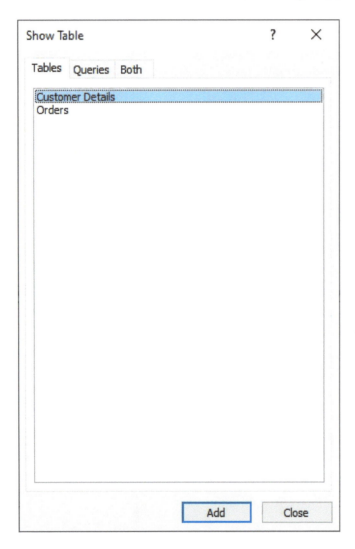

3. Select **Customer Details** and click on the **Add** button

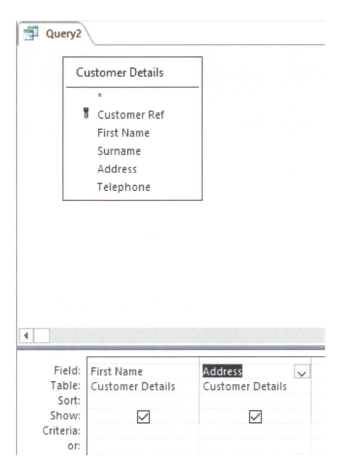

4. Click and drag fields from the **Customer Details** table onto the **Query Grid**

5. For **Criteria**, enter "Henry"

6. On the **Design** tab in the **Results** group, click on **Run**

7. The record containing "Henry" will be displayed

8. Save the query as 'Customer' and close it

© Conor Jordan 2020

Query Design

A query can extract information from two separate tables. The user can specify what information they want displayed within those tables.

1. On the **Create** tab in the **Queries** group, select **Query Design**

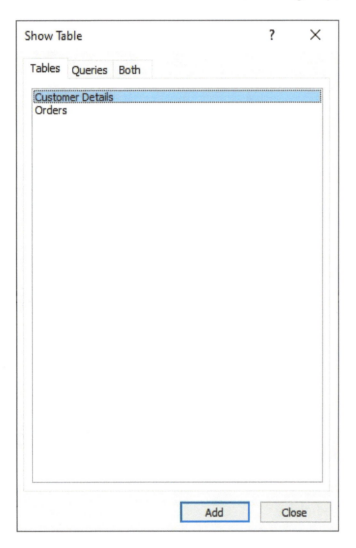

2. Select both the **Customer Details** and **Orders** tables and click on **Add**
3. Click and drag **Customer Ref**, **First Name** and **Surname** fields from the **Customer Details** table

Field:	Customer Ref	First Name	Surname	Order Date
Table:	Customer Details	Customer Details	Customer Details	Orders
Sort:				
Show:	☑	☑	☑	☑
Criteria:				
or:				

4. Click and drag the **Order Date** from the **Orders** table

5. In the **Results** group, click on the **Run** button
6. The results of the **Query** will be shown

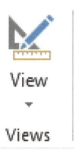

7. Click on the **Design View** button to return to **Query Design View**
8. Click on the **Order Date** field and choose **Order Ref** from the drop-down list
9. **Run** the query to view the results
10. Right-click on the **Query** tab and choose **Save** naming it **Order Query**
11. Right-click on the **Query** tab and choose **Close**

Criteria & Sorting

Queries can be organised so that when certain criteria are met, that is what will be displayed. The results of a query can also be sorted in ascending alphabetical order for instance. These are useful features that allows the user to specify what information will be shown and sort that information in the way the user wants.

1. Open the **Orders** query by right-clicking on the **Query** in the **All Access Objects pane** and choosing **Open**

2. In the **Criteria** box beneath **Surname** type in **Dunne**

Field:	Surname
Table:	Customer Details
Sort:	
Show:	☑
Criteria:	"Dunne"
or:	

3. **Run** the Query

4. The records for Stephen Dunne are shown

5. Return to the **Query Design** view

6. Under Dunne, type in Jones in the **Or** text box

7. **Run** the Query

8. This will display either Dunne or Jones

9. Click on the **Sort** drop-down box in the Surname field

10. Choose **Descending**

11. Run the **Query**

12. The records will be shown in descending order by **Surname**

13. Right-click on the query tab header and select **Save**

14. Name the **Query Sort**

15. Click **OK**

16. In the **First Name** field, type *n

17. This is a wildcard that will show any First Name records ending in N

18. Run the Query

19. Add the **Order Ref** to the query

20. For the **Criteria**, type in >220

21. Run the **Query**

22. This will show all **Order Ref** numbers above those starting with 8

Editing a Query

A query can be edited to show certain information according to the needs of the user. Columns can be included or deleted depending on what needs to be displayed in a query.

1. Select the **Surname** field

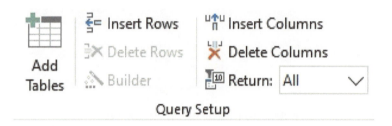

2. In the **Query Setup** group, select **Delete Columns**
3. The column has now been deleted
4. Click on the top of the **First Name** column and drag it to the right to move the field name
5. Click on the **Checkbox** beneath **Surname** to hide a field when a query is run
6. Click on it again to unhide the field name when a query is run
7. Save the query and keep it open

Not Criteria

Information displayed within a query can be specified to not include some information. This is used by implementing the Not Criteria in a query. The user will enter in **Not** before a specific term to exclude that term from the query

1. In the **Surname** field, enter **"Not Dunne"** as the criteria
2. **Run** the Query
3. This will show all of the records that are not Dunne

And Queries

Information shown in a query can include details between certain values. This is useful when the user wants to display ranges of data within a query.

1. In the **Order Ref** field enter **Between** 200 **And** 220 as the **Criteria**
2. **Run** the Query
3. This will show values between both of those numbers
4. **Delete** the contents of the **Criteria** for the **Order Ref** field
5. In the **Order Date** field, enter **>=01/01/2019 And <=01/01/2020** as the **Criteria**
6. This will show all of the orders that were placed in 2019

Printing a Query

A query can be printed to provide the user with a hard copy of the information extracted from the database. This is useful when the user wants to analyse the information that is relevant to their purpose.

1. With the **Order Query** open, click on the **File** tab
2. Choose **Print** from the list of options
3. Choose **Print**

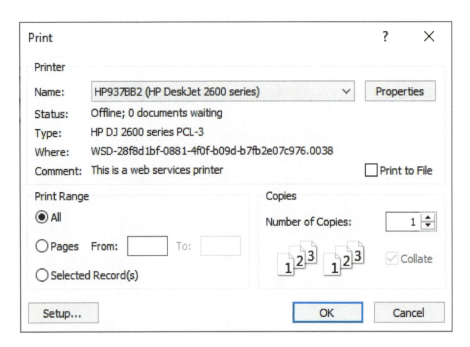

4. Click **OK**
5. The query will now be printed
6. Close the query after it has been printed

Deleting a Query

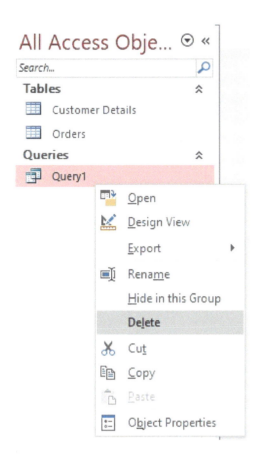

1. On the **All Access Objects** pane, right-click on a **Query**

2. Select **Delete**

3. Choose **Yes**

4. This will delete the selected **Query**

Revision Section 7

1. Open the 'Client Orders' database
2. Create a query based on the **Customer Details** and **Orders** tables
3. Include the **Customer Ref, First Name** fields from the **Customer Details** table and **Order Date** and **Order Ref** from the **Orders** table
4. Sort the query by **First Name** ascending
5. Specify criteria that will only show an **Order Ref** between 220 and 222
6. Set criteria so that only the **First Name** column will display the records from 'Sarah' or 'Henry'
7. Hide the **First Name** field in the query
8. Run the query
9. Save the query as 'Orders'
10. Print a copy of the query
11. Delete the query from the database
12. Close the database

Section 8 – Reports

Create a Report

A report presents information from a query or table in a printable format. Calculations can be performed and information can be displayed in a range of different ways. This allows the user to present data in an easy to understand manner.

1. Open the 'Sales' database
2. Select the **Sales Figures** table
3. On the **Create** tab in the **Reports** group, select **Report**

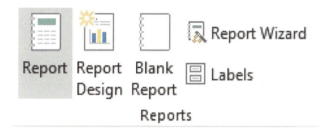

4. Save the report as **Annual Sales**
5. Select the 'Munster Sales' **Query**
6. In the **Reports** group, select **Report**
7. A report based on the query will be produced
8. Scroll down to view the report
9. Save the **Report** as **Munster Report**
10. Right-click on the **Report Tab** and choose **Close**
11. Leave the database open

Report Wizard

The report wizard allows users to create reports based on what information they want to compile in a report.

1. Select the **Sales Figures** table
2. On the **Create** in the **Reports** group, select **Reports Wizard**

3. Click on the double arrow to select all available fields
4. Click on **Next**
5. Group the Report by **Sales** by selecting it and clicking on the right-facing arrow
6. Click on **Next**
7. **Sort** the Report in **Ascending** order
8. Click on **Summary Options**
9. Click on the **Avg** checkbox to calculate the average amount of **Sales**
10. Click **OK**

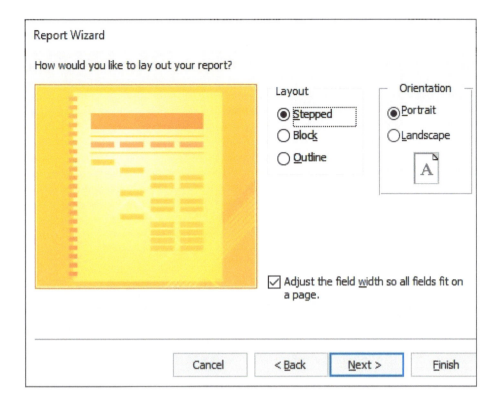

11. Leave the settings as they are and click on Next

12. Name the Report **Sales** and click **Finish**

13. View the report in **Layout View**

14. The report will contain all of the information specified in the wizard setup

15. Leave the report open

Modifying a Report

Details within a report can be modified according to the needs of the user. This is helpful when certain information needs to be displayed.

1. View the report in **Design View**
2. Click to the left of the **First Name** field in the **Design** area and drag it to the left
3. This will show the **First Name** field to the left of the report
4. Switch to **Design View**
5. Click on the **First Name** field
6. On the **Home** tab in the **Font** group, centre align the field
7. Click and drag beneath the **Page Footer.** This will reveal the **Report Footer**
8. On the **Design** tab in the **Controls** group, select **Label**

Controls

9. Create a **Label** in the **Report Footer**
10. Type **Total Sales** into the text box
11. Preview the report to see the changes made
12. Leave the report open

Calculations in Reports

Many calculations can be applied using the report wizard while others can be performed within the report after the wizard is finished. This involves adding a text box which will contain a calculation. All calculations begin with an = sign and field names are contained within square brackets. The Sum function and the Count function can be used to calculate figures within a report.

1. Switch to **Design View**
2. On the **Design** tab in the **Controls** group, select a **Text Box**
3. Click and drag to create a **Text Box** in the **Report Footer**
4. Delete the **Label** that was included with the **Text Box**
5. Enter in the following information into the **Text Box:**

=Sum([Sales])

6. This will add the total number of sales in the report
7. Switch to **Report View** to see the changes made
8. Save the report and leave it open

Printing a Report

When the design of a report is completed, the view is in preview. This allows the user to view how the report will appear when printed and whether all fields will be shown. If they are not, formatting and editing can be carried out in the Layout or Design View.

1. View the report in **Print Preview**
2. In the **Page Layout** group, select **Page Setup**

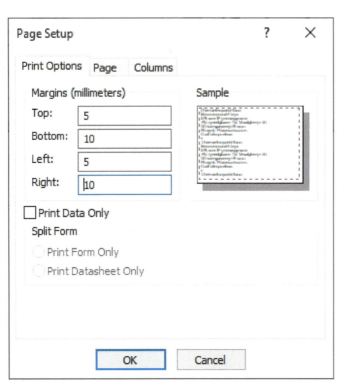

3. Set the **Margins** to 5mm for the Top and Left, 10mm for the Bottom and Right
4. Click **OK**
5. Click on the **Page** tab

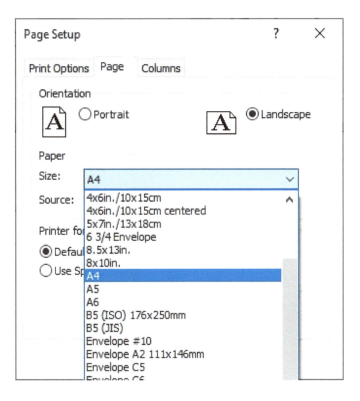

6. Set the **Orientation** to **Landscape**

7. Change the **Paper Size** to **A4**

8. Click **OK**

9. Click on the **Print** button

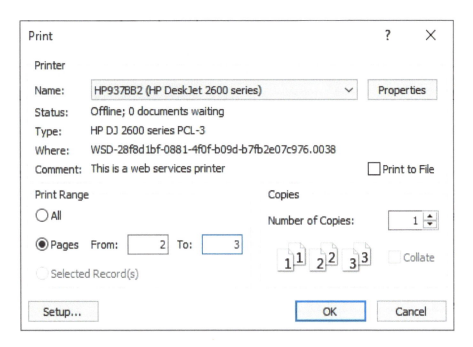

10. Under **Print Range** choose **All** to print all of the **Report**

11. Or choose **Pages** and select what pages you want to print

12. Click **OK**

Deleting a Report

When a report is no longer needed, it can be deleted. Once you delete a report, it cannot be retrieved so make sure that the report is definitely not required before deleting it.

1. In the **All Access Objects** pane, right-click on the report

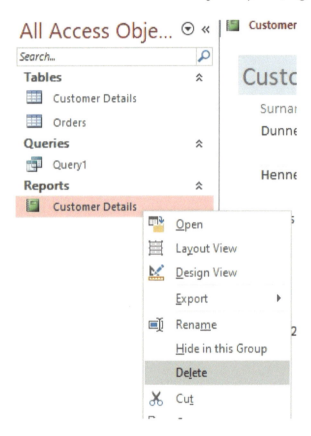

2. Choose **Delete**
3. Click **Yes**

Exporting Data

Data can be exported as a spreadsheet, a text file, an XML file and a PDF file. This data can then be used in different software packages that support these formats. You may have completed a report in Access and want to edit the information in Excel. This can be achieved by exporting the data for Excel.

1. Open the **Sales Figures** table

2. On the **External Data** tab in the **Export** group, select **Excel**

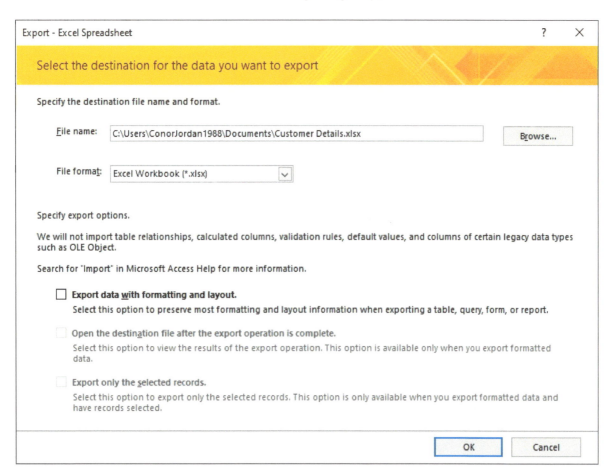

3. Click on the **Browse** button and choose a location to save the file
4. Click on the **Export Data With Formatting And Layout** checkbox
5. Click **OK**
6. Click on the **Close** button
7. The file has now been exported as a spreadsheet format that can be used in Excel
8. Leave the database open

Exporting as a Text File

Data within a report can be exported as a text file. This can be exported using the original formatting and layout so the style of the report remains the same. This can then be opened using another software package such as Notepad.

1. Open the **Orders** table
2. On the **External Data** tab in the **Export** group, click on **Text File**

3. Choose a location to save the **Text File**
4. Click on the **Export Data With Formatting And Layout** checkbox
5. Click **OK**

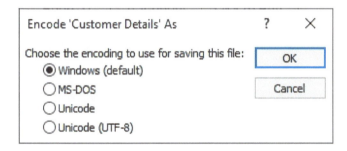

6. Choose **Windows (default)**
7. Click **OK**
8. Click on the **Close** button
9. Repeat the same process with the **Report Query**

XML Format

Data can be exported in XML format which is in the form of Extensible Markup Language. This type of file can be opened using Notepad in Windows systems or TextEdit on a Mac computer.

1. On the **External Data** tab in the **Export** group, click on **XML File**

2. Choose a location to save the file
3. Click **OK**

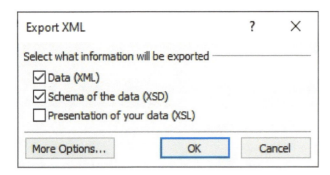

4. Click **OK**
5. Click on the **Close** button

Export as PDF

A PDF file is a Portable Document Format file that is used to display documents in an electronic form independent of software, hardware or operating systems they are viewed on. It is typically used for read-only documents and are commonly used for scanned documents, manuals and application forms.

1. Open the **Sales Figures Report**
2. On the **External Data** tab in the **Export** group, click on **PDF or XPS**

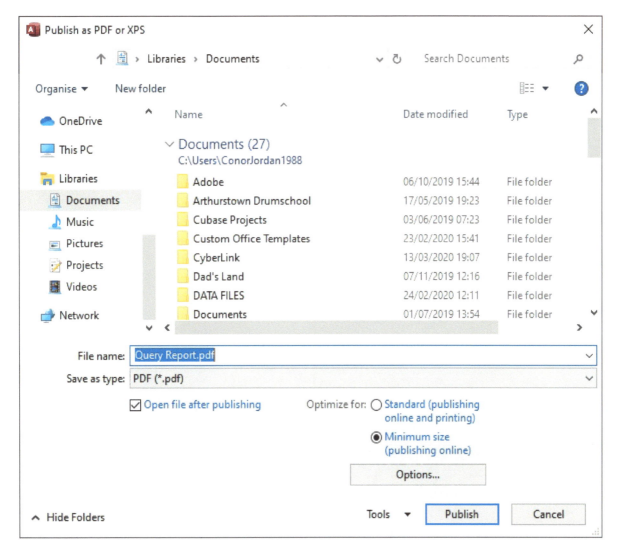

3. Choose a location to create the **PDF** document

4. Click on **Publish**

5. You can view the **PDF** document

6. Click on the **Close** button

Revision Section 8

1. Open the 'Sales' database

2. Create a query that displays the annual sales for **Leinster** called **Leinster Query'**

3. Create a **Leinster Sales** report based on the **Leinster Query** using the **Report Wizard**

4. Sort the report by **First Name** in ascending order

5. Calculate the **Average** amount of sales in the report

6. Include a **Label** in the **Page Footer** containing the text 'Sales Figures Leinster'

7. Create a **Text Box** in the **Report Footer** with a calculation that will find the total amount of sales in the report and enter the **Label** with the text 'Total Sales'

8. Print the report in **Landscape** view and set the **Margins** at 10mm for the Top and Bottom margins and 5mm for the Left and Right margins

9. Use an A4 size for the paper used

10. Export the data contained within the report in **Excel Workbook** format

11. Delete the report created

12. Save the database as 'Report' and close it